Comfort and Joy for a Hurting World

Written by Jan Asleson
Illustrated/Design Layout by Jan Asleson

Copyright © 2018

ISBN 9780692088043

Library of Congress Control Number: 2019902475

Printed in the United States of America by Ingram Spark/Lightning Source

Published by Spirit Wings Designs 2018
daslpacker55@yahoo.com

Visit at www.spiritwingsdesigns.com

Comfort and Joy
for
A Hurting World

Created by

Jan Asleson

He is the God of All Comfort

2 Corinthians 1:3

Comfort - Freedom from worry or disappointment, relief in affliction; to soothe, console, solace

Joy - The emotion of great happiness, delight, pleasure

This book is dedicated to my fellow sojourners through this dark and stormy world who have also found comfort and joy in God's great love. To David, my knight in shining armor, no not perfect, but almost. Sheryl, Steve & Ruth, Patty, Melanie, Kathleen, Barbara, Amber, Michele, Marge, Deniese, Vicki, Debra, your encouragement and support have sustained me in the fray... and given me courage to press on. And most of all, Jesus, without You there would be no hope at all.

God, the great Creator,

will lead you

like a horse in the desert;

you will not stumble

For He knows all

the birds of the sky

Like cattle going down to a peaceful valley;

He will give you rest

All the flowers of

the fields are His

And He gives food to

the little birds that call

He knows every

sparrow that falls

So look at the beauty of

the lilies; do not worry

For you are worth

far more than many sparrows

Because He knows every hair

on your head; do not fear

He will gather you in

His arms and carry

you close to His Heart

He is the God

of all Comfort!

Everyone has a story, created by thousands of events in each individual life. Those events define and make each person who they are, who they will become, based on their experiences and what they believe about them. Most events are day-to-day happenings that we all experience, just life in general. Others are life-changing. It is those life-changing events that can mold and shape us for good or for destruction. This book is my story.

As I sit down to write this I ask myself, "Where do I begin? How much do I share?" My desire is to not bog you the reader down but to encourage you in your journey. Growing up, my reality was fraught with negative events. Those negative events told me that I was not valuable as a human being and that I never would be. I believed that my value was based on my performance and I fell short so often. Because I didn't value and respect myself, I didn't expect anyone else to either. I made a lot of wrong choices in my pursuit to be accepted. Some of those choices have affected my life until this day. Was I a victim? When you are oppressed, mistreated, injured or destroyed, you are a victim, whether as a consequence of your own choices or the choices and actions of others. We have all been victims of someone or some event at some time in our lives.

I don't want to get into all the miry details of those negative life-defining events that were shaping me, or to give them more importance than is needed, but I will skim over them as a skipped stone over water. It is not always wise to tell all...however, I was raped three times, had an abortion, married a physically abusive man, divorced him after living in adultery with a married man who practiced and involved me in occultic spirit-ism, attempted suicide, and more. There, I said it. Did I feel lost, confused and adrift? Shamed, unlovable and dirty? Yes. Those events happened to me from the time I left home at the age of 16 until I was 26. Then, I met Jesus.

Growing up going to church had left a negative impression on me. Much was said about God and His love but I rarely saw or experienced it personally. Instead, the message was follow the rules and keep your mouth shut and all will be well. I really wanted to believe and know this God of love they talked about. At the age of eight I even went down the aisle of the church and and asked God to forgive me and save me. I was baptized.

It's not that my parents didn't love me. Wow, parenting! The most long-term, learn-as-you-go job you can have. God was and is the Perfect Creator, but look at Adam and Eve! So, from 16 to 26, I tripped along often falling headlong into poor choices in my search for exceptance and love as so many of us have done. But God. I really did want to know if He was real and who He was. In 1983, as I was about to make a momentous poor decision in my quest for God which involved occultism, God intervened. A revelation came to me that maybe Jesus was really truly real. And if He was I wanted to know, so I said "Jesus, if you are real, show me." And He did. I didn't see Him materialize before me or hear Him talk to me but an overwhelming Love and Peace and Joy enveloped me. As my earthly Dad explains it, it was a "Spiritual Orgasm." I hope that's not too explicit! For the first time in my life memory, I knew I was truly loved and accepted, not based upon my performance but based upon what Jesus gave up for me. The greatest life-defining event of my life had just happened!

From that moment on, my life changed. I knew that I was loved and forgiven.

One life-giving event stacked up against 26 years of loss and pain. In fact, so much emotional pain that I mentally lost years between elementary school and high school. I know, I know, I'm going on about it but even though I had a paradigm shift, I was afraid. So afraid and I didn't even know it. But I'm getting ahead of myself.

When I was 27, I met a wonderful Christian man and married him. Before meeting Jesus, my life was in great disrepair. I bore 2 children from 2 different men, and neither of them were living with me. My wrong choices not only effected me but my children. That's the problem with sin, whether unintentional or intentional. That's what sin does. It creates harm to the sinner and also those around the sinner. Over time, my life improved and became more stable, not only because of my relationship with God but also because of a loving husband and fellowship with other supportive people. My thinking and believing was changing bit by bit. I still had periods of feeling like I had to prove myself and measure up to others' expectations of me. As time went on the old pressures of performance resurfaced, especially when I felt that I had let others down or disappointed them. I became defensive and easily hurt and offended even though I knew it was wrong. I mistakenly believed that if I did everything "right," life would go my way. Little did I know how wrong I was!

In 2006 my mom died in a tragic car accident. It stunned us all. My husband and I moved in with my dad to help him, giving up the property and home we were building an hours drive away. We put most of our possessions in storage and in 2007, when the local river flooded the town, we lost 80% of them. In 2009, I was diagnosed with a rare aggressive ovarian cancer. Again, I was devastated, but God brought me through with the help of a loving husband, family and friends. Even though I knew that God was with me and had brought me through so much, I still felt a conflict deep inside that scared me.

In the fall of 2016, I experienced a major life-changing event. I had really been pushing myself to finish a couple work projects, burning the midnight oil. I was really tired and stressed and my body was somewhat run down. I woke up one morning, sat down with my coffee and had a panic attack. Fear and panic are companions that can strike when you are least prepared. Off and on during the day, I would be overwhelmed with fear. This went on for several days. In the past when I felt overwhelmed I would walk in the woods around my home, and the beauty of God's creation would soothe me, comfort me, bring me joy. The birds, deer, trees and sky would remind me of God's love for me and settle me. But not this time. Nothing helped. I was so physically distraught that I couldn't eat. Nothing seemed to work. I even went to my doctor and he gave me some medication to help calm me-not what I wanted to do. I wanted to be able to get through this without drugs but I was desperate. I couldn't even hear God.

The event happened at my church on a Sunday morning many days later. I had been praying and asking God why I was experiencing this pain. During the worship service, God spoke to me and asked me what I was afraid of. I immediately knew that I was afraid of the cancer coming back. He asked me to release the fear to Him. He then showed me that even though I had recognized and identified the loss, grief and pain in my past, I had never released it but had shoved it down deep inside of myself. It was like a volcano and it had blown. As I sat there, thoughts and images of the events of my past came flooding to me and God said, "Release the events, the grief, the pain." I held out my hands and gave it all to God. My whole body sighed and relaxed, the tension gone.

What He showed me next surprised me. Not only had I been tormented by the past, but also by the thought of more events of loss and pain happening to me in the present and future, and fear about how I would respond to those events. I had been so fractured deep inside that the thought of more was insurmountable to me. As I asked God to forgive me for not trusting Him with my past, present and future, He showed me that it was out of His deep love for me and all of His children that He created all the beauty in the world, that beauty that I so often gazed on and drank of. I was shown the richness of His love for me and for others. Since that event, stress, pressure and fear still creep in at times, but I know how to identify it and release it to God. When I do, His Comfort and Joy come flooding in, that Joy of knowing His great love for me.

If you can identify with my story, my prayer for you is that you find that same Comfort and Joy in God, the one who created you that I have. I pray that the art and verses open your heart to His love for you. If you don't know Jesus, I invite you to experience Him as I have. It's really quite simple. First acknowledging your need for Him and that you have sinned against Him. In the Bible, Romans 3:23 states that "All have sinned and fallen short of the glory of God." (NIV) Pray this prayer with me:

God, I come to you asking you to forgive me of my sins. I believe that Jesus died on the cross for me and I ask that you, Jesus, come into my heart and take my life. I freely give it to you to do as you desire.

If you prayed this prayer, I encourage you to find others that have given themselves to Jesus so that you can learn and grow in a relationship with Him. It really isn't about following rules; it's about a relationship with the One who made you.

And now to all of you that have chosen Jesus as He has chosen you, I encourage you that when suffering, trouble, loss, hurt and hard events come, that you identify them and release them. Jesus said in John 16:33 "In this world you will have trouble. But take heart! I have overcome the world."

Even now you can experience that Freedom, Comfort and Joy in Him. Pray with me:

Lord Jesus, show me the events and experiences in my life that have created conflict, fear and distrust in me.

Take time to wait on God and write down what He shows you.

Heart Thoughts and Reflections

Pray this Prayer of Release with me:

Father God, in Jesus' name I release all the hurt, pain, grief, suffering, loss and anything else that is creating conflict in my very being. I give you any anger, bitterness or unforgiveness towards anyone including myself. I receive your forgiveness, love, comfort and joy, your peace into my heart, my mind and my body. I release all trauma from these events that could have affected me physically or mentally. I praise you and thank you for being my Healer, my Deliverer, my Saviour. Amen

Now my prayer for you: Dear Lord, I pray for this one who has come to you in faith, sincerity and humility. Thank you for saving them and loving them, for comforting them and showing them your joy and delight for them. I ask that you make them strong in their love and faith towards you, that they will experience you and all that you have for them in deeper and more meaningful ways. Amen!

Enter into the Joy of the Lord!

Jan Asleson
Author/Illustrator

My designs are inspired by a desire to share with others the beauty I see around me. My passion is to encourage others through my artistic mediums to not give up on their dreams, to recognize the blessings all around them and to know that there is always hope. In my life journey to know who I am, I've discovered that what I've come to recognize as true art comes from the greatest Artist of all, God. I believe that when we connect with each other on a heart to heart level, our lives can be changed for the good. I hope that in some way my creations will touch your heart.

I enjoy creating beauty through mediums of paintings, metal works of jewelry, silk art and natural textiles, leather work, portraiture, prints and greeting cards.

I live in Southeast Kansas with my husband David, two horses and a dog. My treasures are my daughter Hannah, my son Cyrus and his wife Stephanie, and my 7 grandchildren: Avery, Landen, Brianna, Eva, Jaxson, Corbin and Xander.

Page 1-2   Isaiah 63:13b   "Like a horse in open country, they did not stumble."

Page 3-4   Psalm 50:11a   "I know every bird in the mountains."

Page 5-6   Isaiah 63:13   "Like cattle that go down to the plain, they were given rest by the Spirit of the Lord."

Page 7-8   Psalm 50:11b   "and the flowers in the fields are mine."

Page 9-10   Psalm 147:9   "He provides food for the cattle and for the birds when they call."

Page 11-12 Matthew 10:29   "Are not two sparrows sold for a penny? Yet not one of them will fall to the ground outside your Father's care."

Page 13-14 Matthew 6:28   "And why do you worry about clothes? See how the flowers of the field grow. They do not labor or spin."

Page 15-16 Luke 12:7b   "Don't be afraid, you are worth more than many sparrows."

Page 17-18 Luke 12:7a   "Indeed, the very hairs of your head are all numbered."

Page 19-20 Isaiah 40:11   "He tends His flock like a shepherd: He gathers the lambs in His arms and carries them close to His heart."

Page 21-22:

2 Corinthians 1:3-5 "Praise be to the God and Father of our Lord Jesus Christ, the Father of compassion and the God of all comfort, who comforts us in all our trouble, so that we can comfort those in any trouble with the comfort we ourselves receive from God. For just as we share abundantly in the sufferings of Christ, so also our comfort abounds through Christ."

Page 1-2   The Arabian Horse originated in the Arabian Peninsula, prominently arid land.

Page 3-4   The Tawny Eagle is a large raptor and can be found throughout southern Africa,
Morocco and southern Arabia. They can live up to 16 years of age.

Page 5-6   The Nguni Cattle breed is prominent in southern Africa. They are known for
their fertility and resistance to diseases.

Page 7-8   Wildflowers are prevalent around the world, and the Whitetail Deer Fawn is found
in North America.

Page 9-10   The American Goldfinch and Knapweed, a short-live perennial plant.

Page 11-12   The Chipping Sparrow is a small bird that often builds its nests in shrubs.

Page 13-14   The Red Anemone, or Poppy Anemone is considered by many Biblical scholars
to be the Lily spoken of in the Bible. It is also the National Flower of Israel.

Page 15-16   The Eurasian Tree Sparrow, also called the German Sparrow is from Asia and has
been introduced in the United States.

Page 17-18   Auburn haired girl with soap bubbles

Page 19-20   Jesus with Ewe and lamb

Page 21-22   Jesus with Lamb

George A Miller (1995). WordNet: A Lexical Database for English
Communications of the ACM Vol. 38, No. 11: 39-41

Christiane Fellbaum (1998, ed.) WordNet: An Electronic Lexical Database. Cambridge, MA: MIT Press.

If you are interested in having me come and speak to your group, or in purchasing art prints from this book, you may contact me at:

Jan Asleson
www.spiritwingsdesigns.com
daslpacker55@yahoo.com

www.ingramcontent.com/pod-product-compliance
Lightning Source LLC
Chambersburg PA
CBHW040403100426